Tilling the Darkness

01 02 03 04 05 27 26 25 24 23

Caitlin Press Inc.
3375 Ponderosa Way
Qualicum Beach, BC V9K 2J8
www.caitlin-press.com

Text design by Sarah Corsie
Cover design by Vici Johnstone
Cover artwork by Meghan Hildebrand
Edited by Anita Lahey
Printed in Canada

Caitlin Press Inc. acknowledges financial support from the Government of Can-
ada and the Canada Council for the Arts, and the Province of British Columbia
through the British Columbia Arts Council and the Book Publisher's Tax Credit.

Library and Archives Canada Cataloguing in Publication

Tilling the darkness / by Susan Braley.
Braley, Susan, author.
Canadiana 20220440859 | ISBN 9781773861067 (softcover)
LCGFT: Poetry.
LCC PS8603.R353 T55 2023 | DDC C811/.6—dc23

Tilling the Darkness

poems by Susan Braley

CAITLIN PRESS 2023

For Gary,

tireless tiller of light

Black ground worked up in the spring, all loam
and vowel: a deeper language
. . . . Dark matter turned
to the understory light.

from "Plow"
in *Ordinary Hours* by Karen Enns

TABLE OF CONTENTS

VIA FEMMINILE

SEEDBED

PREFACE

I was born into a family of eleven on 150 acres of clay-loam in Southern Ontario. This setting—the seasons vivid over the fields, birth and death sudden in the barn—honed my imagination from a young age. As the fourth child and the second-eldest daughter in this traditional Catholic home, I grew up quickly, charged with classic "women's work" in the house, including child care. *Tilling the Darkness* explores how I navigated the inequities of gender roles on the farm and at church, and later in adulthood, and how I came to appreciate the complex, bountiful legacy of my early rural life.

Once you read the poems in *Tilling the Darkness*, they will be complete.

Only One Round

The furrow behind his plough
clean and true, ploughshares
lifting at the moment
fresh-till met the headland

My father, a cartographer.

His eyes warmed as I climbed up
sat on the red fender
wider than the length of my arm
I reached over to grasp the edge of his seat

He didn't need to say
Only one round
it was too loud to talk anyhow

The tractor surged, bore down,
guttural. Thrum of metal
in the soles of my feet

The narrow head of the tractor
pressed up the slope,
like a lead horse, imperious
through rubble and muck

I tightened my grip over bumps
(Dad didn't reach over
to steady me)
he sat sideways, calm,
eye on the plough

Thin discs slit the ground,
shares carved deep into clay
lifted the underside up

the furrow slices
gleaming, dark
earth pelts

On our return down the slope
the field stretched acres-wide
on either side, like the open-air
theatre I'd seen in a book

black furrows on our left
bleached stubble on our right
like great banners laid down.
                Gulls swooped

cried out, proprietary.
Rogue wind in our faces
clouds mounted high in the sky
gun-powder grey, weighty

He dropped me off, a little smile,
then his back   *bank loans*
mind likely churning   *calf*
with pneumonia   bank loans
The tractor roared on

                            The air so still
close to the ground

Along the furrow,
curved mounds laid bare

I searched their seams for
glass button, blue bottle, broken plate.

UNDERSTORY

The Hired Man

Beside the thick steers,
his body looked wasted.
Breath clouds hung
in fetid air. Alone

in the bottom of the barn,
he scraped muck from the pen.
Hoof and boot sunk in sullied straw.
Ankles pushing through treacle.

I watched him climb to the loft,
the ladder's spine firm in his grip.
I followed, soft-shoed,
giddy in the dome of the mow.

The clean straw like the inverted bowl
of a chalice. Chute to the steers' pen
a shaft of light.

I gripped the ladder's highest rung.
Straw gleamed in the hired man's arms.
He moved to the chute, let go his load,
leaned into the swirl of gold,
and was gone.

I crept to the brink.
He wasn't there, maimed or whole,
only the cattle who stood together
belly to belly. I climbed down.

He wasn't there.
I looked the cattle in the eyes. Dark glass.
Bits of yellow clung to their sides.

In the air above our heads,
dust motes swirled.

To Bring a Girl

My mother had three sons,
one by one delivered in September.
Just for Dad on New Year's Eve,
three times in a row, she'd brandished
an antique revolver, wore her Annie
Get Your Gun costume. Sipped Yuletide punch.
Last time, he'd even caught her on camera.
Those three sons grew fast,
and one by one, wandered off.

In the year before I came, she refused
the Annie get-up.
Nine months before my arrival,
Mom lined her empty basket
with an old skirt, apple-green, covered
in trilliums (flowers too rare to pluck).

Took Dad to a local market, passed
him Early Girl tomatoes, pressed
the grassy scent of round-bottomed
pears to his nose, tucked the violet
oblong of eggplant into the crook
of his elbow. They came home,
the basket overflowing. That night,
he gestured out the bedroom window. *Look,*
he said, *the old moon is holding*
the new moon in its arms.

Pretty Stones

Outside, my brothers drive tractors
in the fields, stretch green
limbs to reach the controls.
Sit up proud.

On hot days, they wear no shirts.
Before dinner, scrub dust
off toasted skin, cover up only to eat.
When they're finished,
I clean the sink—on repeat,
like the Dutch girl on the cleanser tin
dwindling to nothing.

In the spring, we girls are sent outside
to follow a wagon
with the boys,
gather rocks
before crops come up.
Briefly essential. No shorts
in case we're seen from the road.

Between fields
we ride on the wagon
my brother pushes me off
—for fun, he says—
when we cross a creek.

We collect pretty stones
—dove-grey granite,
once molten—take them home.

The Cream and the Milk

1

As if the moon was always full,
the house roiled. The baby cried,
fat bubbled, grime multiplied, the washer
thrashed. Math texts glued with toast-and-jam.
For us girls, tasks piled—rampant, fecund—
like windfall under apple trees.
No time for Mom to wipe
smudges from her glasses.

Morning and night, she ran
across the gravel yard between
house and barn to help with milking.
I envied her, offered to scrub the clotted
pails if she'd let me go in her place.

2

The barn hummed with the separator
skimming cream from the milk.
On cue, the cows stood in their stalls,
cement swept clean beneath their hooves.
Metal restraints circled their necks.
Stainless steel cups sucked their teats.
Squeezed, chugged, clicked.
I moved the teat cups
from cow to docile cow,
their hides warm, udders soft cheeks.
At the far end of the barn, my father sang
"Faded Love" by Patsy Cline.
The boys doled out the feed.
The cows chewed, flicked tails.
Minerva, Rutheena, Gem.

3

But Bonnie.
She sidestepped, kicked,
swiped at my hand with a back hoof.
She burrowed her muzzle in the trough,
drove her nose high, tossed
corn and hay overhead. Snapped
open the frame around her neck.
I knew what my mother would say
—*close it, be quick.* But I stood, ran
my hand along Bonnie's spine.
When I reached her face, I brushed away
the alfalfa scattered on her eyes.

Summer Corn

July

My father's cropping train—
tractor-harvester-wagon-wagon-blower
—darkens the yard.
At last he aims it out the lane.

Light pours into the space left behind

        my mother young   legs free of stockings

            we girls sneakerless

        long table free of plates, silverware

    grilled cheese sandwiches, ironed thin

      strawberries plucked from the flat, scarlet

        seeping between our fingers

           Mom sits and laughs at our stories

        tells us *Your dad was so quiet when we went out,*

         I did the talking for us both

Outside in the pasture,

        Holstein cows float

                daubs of paint in the still heat.

I go to the fields

        to stand between rows of young corn

                touch the tasseled heads

      small cobs swaddled

            in grass-green, blonde-silk

strands emerging at their tips

               all poised to ripen.

August

The air thickens like soured milk.
Trucks, combine, wagons clog our wheat field.

I pick my way
      ankles stubble-scratched
      through windrows
      wheat laid low
to deliver water.

The rattle of machinery stills.

My brothers' faces masked with dust
mouths wet gashes.
The men pass the jug.

Then the rattle again
      my voice swept with the wheat
      into the combine's teeth.

We girls wedge another leaf into the table.
My father leads the hired men in for lunch.

Mom at the stove, white slip-strap sliding out of her housedress, down her arm.
Men's talk consumes the room, rumbling like trucks.
My brothers summon their best low pitch.

> We stand at the counter
> converse under our breath
> spoon peach crumble into bowls.

After dishes, Mom takes us to the field.
The corn plants twice my height, some cobs hard, petrified muscle.
Leaves coarse, silk darkened, wiry as horse-hair stuffing. Some cobs swell
with fungus. Smut, we call it.

Mom twists good cobs off with one swift turn,
drops them into a sack. The stalks empty, desolate.
Mom's eyes—swollen from ragweed, she says.
She sends me after the little ones, they race down the rows,
directionless. The leaves—tangled, dry—block my way.

I can find no sign of the place,
where just weeks before, all was
green and just beginning.

House of Siblings

I sweep, wipe
as they caper by.
In the blur,
one sister's torso stretched,
another smaller, no sprout
of breasts. Two more
with kitten wrists twirl
together on the tilting floor.

Out the window:
two brothers, shirtless,
stand on the teeter-totter,
bodies snaking, black hair,
new, under acrobat arms.

Not long ago,
when they wrestled, I'd catapult
into the churn of salt-flesh
and bone, my limbs theirs
theirs mine, pulses cresting.
My body gathers itself
to bolt—

but I'm called away
to change the baby.
When I stoop to settle him,
he searches my chest,
expecting.

The Water Trough

Outside the barn, a water trough stood in the corner of the fenced cattle yard. The trough had rough cement walls, its dark surface the size of a grave. When the copper-red Shorthorns, thick as freighters, finished drinking, my brothers raced plastic boats on this black sea, their small bodies pressed against the trough wall seeping in the heat. Once, when they tired of their boats, my older brother scooped up a grey kitten and dropped it into the water. The kitten flailed, fought. Its head slipped under, then reappeared. Silent, my brothers watched. Our grandfather drowned kittens at the trough if they were sick or too many. At the far edge, the kitten scrabbled to lift itself out, pink flesh visible through plastered fur. My younger brother thrust his hand under its soft belly. "I wasn't going to let it sink," the older one said.

Cleansed

1

airborne
high over the hopper
Dad drops me lightly inside
its ripe-green walls
sky a hot blue square above

it's easier to sit than stand
the wheat sloping, shifting
sand dune (though I don't know
the word *dune* yet)
wheat kernels rounded
each one with a seam down the middle
a tiny eye squeezed shut

a smaller brother and sister land beside me
we pull off our sneakers—blue, red, black—

the red horse-head pipe swings over the hopper's lip

a leap in the combine's throat

stream of wheat pouring down
we lie on our backs, thrust our feet
into the thick gold rain (we don't know
waterfall)

we whoop

wheat tickles our soles, lights up our legs
(we don't know about the washing of feet,
the prodigal cleansed, welcomed home)

kernels' split-second stings
sudden weight at our waists

the rain stops

we're half-covered, half-laughing
we want to go again

Dad looks in, grins *Time
to find your shoes, come out*
we don't know children could drown
in wheat

only one blue shoe for him to recover
on the granary's conveyor belt

2

in the yard, the black
conveyer belt, not
to be touched
(I got three blood blisters
on my fingertips)

a long grey blur running fast
from hopper to granary
kernels chopped en route
into feed for cattle

in the house
if we cared to see (and we did)
a piece of the belt, cut
to the length of a ruler
but twice its width

stored in the middle drawer
in the kitchen, under
gloves never worn
plaid head warmers
for winter storm days

the belt lay heavy on our hands
carcass of tight woven fibres
cover black rubber

the black faded to grey
clouded with whitish powder
crushed-grain dust, maybe
or wear, years of use

we called it the strap

did my father's father hand it down
along with the farm
an instrument of the era

my friend on the next farm
showed me the stripped stump
in their woodshed, where
she was made to lie
for her punishments

did my father, conscripted
to take over the farm,
made to give up machine design,
stand at his workbench
cutting, trimming
while we were at school

the child is father to the man

we never held the belt for long—

the one who bore its blows

the rest of us
a mute Greek chorus
kneeling at the kitchen chairs—

after supper, we prayed the rosary aloud
my mother assigned us our parts
one child leading, ten beads
Hail Mary full of grace
the rest replying
Holy Mary, Mother of God,
pray for us sinners

3

my father preferred to be silent
that day, my brother preferred to be silent

my mother insisted, three times, her voice rising
my brother did not pray

this is hard to write about
I loved my father.

He lunged across the kitchen
to the middle drawer
he, a thundercloud towering,
his arm, the strap raining down
my brother darting, cowering

only the sound of a fly, legs caught in sticky paper

my father, strap limp in his hand,
dumbfounded

the rest of us finished the prayers
our voices high like live wires

Measuring Tape

I stand at my mother's
dresser mirror,
see my lank, short hair.
Not curly as it used to be
(after pink-bristle rollers).
Not long—I have it cropped
like a boy's.

Two shy buds nudge the front
of my polyester blouse,
like the soft
seedling nubs pushing up
in the field.
Foreign. But not.
I button my blouse up to the neck.

On the dresser, my mother's
hairpins, lipstick, compact.
My sister's *be cherry!*
nail polish. In the drawers,
slips, stockings, an elastic
rubber girdle for "reducing
unwanted flesh."
Underwired bras stacked,
one on the next.

*

When I reach down
for my running shoes,
my sister tackles me,
sits on my legs. I squirm, try
to throw off her weight, shout
for her to stop. She grabs
my wrists, holds them down.
She smirks. She's not playing.

Next, Mom's face
appears. *Come now*, she says.
She wrestles a measuring tape
around my chest. *You can't
go out like this anymore.*

In summer heat, I used to
jump from the porch
topless. Now if Mom catches me,
she stays at the screen door until
I am covered again.

Held Down

Outside the pig barn
I find a knife in the chipped
enamel dish once used in the kitchen.

I don't go into that barn often.
The pigs' high-pitched squeals. Busy-
bodies, blunt-nosed, coarse-haired,
pressed against my brothers' legs
at feeding. The loose waste
rife with ammonia.

That day, my father at the sink
scrubs his hands hard.
My uncle slumps
on the wood box near the stove,
face white as salt.

In the pig barn
the pigs are voiceless,
milling in ragged circles.
Scrotums sliced, bleeding,
slack where testicles would be.
(No one buys whole-male pork.)

We were there, my brother tells me later.
We had to hold the pigs down.

We girls in the house ironing,
canning pears, studying.

That morning, my oldest brother

did not ride away
(as he so often did)
on his filly, wiry,
dusk-grey, wild
as a twister

he caught his foot
in the automatic unloader
high in the silo
he cried out
for our father

who climbed the long
steel ladder
guided him, his mangled
foot, down

our father held
my brother then
and wept

Archived

the barn on its knees
skeletal, one peak still erect
the rest a vast firepit
lava-red field

men in dark clusters
action figures
watching a giant expire

my brothers work, feverish,
with uncles, cousins,
neighbours
heave pigs out of windows
lead the reeling horse
down the barn hill
pry the cream separator
from the milkhouse floor
plant it like a flag on the lawn

I race to the stable
where my father is freeing the cows, flames
crackling in the mow overhead

he urges each cow,
a hand on her flank,
down the cement aisle
to the open gate
his silence calms them

I try to help
beg him to leave

his silence tells me to go

when the fire catches high in the barn

roars like a freak wind
through hay piled to the rafters

when the mow glows like a slotted lantern

when spark showers arc toward the house

ladybird, ladybird, fly away home—

we are sent to my grandmother's
the little ones and family papers in our arms
we women, the archive

on our return

cows tethered
in the driveshed
among the tractors

pigs corralled
in the little field

a firefighter
a kind of gladiator
sprays his hose
douses the buildings
left standing

the house dark, damp
but itself
I feel something
like reverence

the wind has dropped, my mother says
it's safe for you to go to bed

she lights a bit of blessed palm

to bring us nearer to God

—your house is on fire, your children shall burn

she has not cried, and won't

we don't either

my sister and I lie in bed
in our clothes, wonder
where the barn cats went
is that smoke in the hall

my eyes have just closed

rush of water on the window
like a body flung against glass

grief trying to arrive

Undersong

I'm at the table,
laminated cloth beneath my elbows,
notebook open, new
HB in my fist.
Mother's dress is sleeveless, white.

Her voice lifts and settles,
steam rising from her iron like breath.

Her words are pictures:
ten china dolls in her aunt's glass case,
her grandmother a runaway at sixty-eight.

I've stopped wanting
to cross the gravel
between house and shop, crouch
with Dad at the tractor's belly, the oil black
blood welling, his fingers swiveling
serpent hoses and soot-coated thermoses.

He tried once to teach me
to catch dropped beats
in the motor's pulse. His eyes
kind, comments few, falling
like low notes on his
steel-toed boots.

On my immaculate page, letters stream
over the sea-blue lines. I make
my mother's sister, still-born,
a waxen queen. I make her laugh.

I hear his wrench tapping
on the tractor. A wrought
bass, a shy, systolic grace.
He's conducting
fuel and air, tuning a small
universe.

CLAY FALLING INTO FURROW

Taking the Waters 1

In a farmhouse down the road,
a Mennonite woman unpinned
her mesh prayer cap,
rested it on plain black shoes.
Her black stockings curled
under leather tongues.
Left them behind her on the cellar stairs.
She disrobed as far as she could
imagine. Placed her toes at
the edge of the cistern. She let herself
fall—or did she spring—
into the dark rectangle
of rainwater. *If only*
she hadn't run out of
medication,
my mother said at her funeral.

Uncle

He'd always liked to play dress-up: collars wide as jumping jacks and bright
ties the colour of mangoes and plantains. He wore these suits to church, and
at parties too, where he whirled sisters and daughters on the dance floor,
a pinwheel in a hurricane. At my cousin's wedding, he bent to greet me,
cinnamon hand on mine, his cleft lip stitched like Raggedy Andy's. Later, I
saw him in photos: once, shirtless, jaw defiant, holding hands with a man on
a hayride, and once, hair white and wild as a prophet's, an infant grandson
clasped to his chest.

When his children were grown, he left home. His wife took scissors to his
suits, chopped them into pieces, tossed them out the bedroom window. Bits
of cloth floated down—herringbone, pinstripe, linen—like the limbs of a
paper doll.

Extramarital Daughter

At March break, the new girls
at our one-room rural school
invite me and my sister to play.

I am nine. We go
to the kitchen table, set for four,
though I see five girls. The mother
at the counter, hair teased high and shiny,
speaks only to the girl in the corner.

Get a move on, Patty, if you know
what's good for you.

Patty stands at the far end of the kitchen
with a pail and a rag.
Margaret, two years older than me,
pours grape Kool-Aid into plastic
teacups. She raises her pinky,
laughs a tight laugh. Sits.
My little sister Fran drinks without
being invited to.
Patty stoops to wet her rag, glances
over at us. Her eyes gloss.

I told you to face the windows.

Fran puts down her cup.
The youngest sister Claire
brings cookies on a plastic plate.
"Dad's favourite," says Margaret.
Claire sits, folds her legs under her.
"She talked back," she says, chin thrust at Patty.
Claire looks like Margaret,
her face round, russet hair wavy.

Patty has moved her pail closer
to us now. Her hands are red.
Her white-blonde hair,
down her back last week,
is cropped short, uneven.

Claire takes apart her cookie. "I wish
I could have a birthday cake like this,"
she announces. "Vanilla *and* chocolate."
"Me too," says Fran. "What about you?"
she asks me. "I don't care," I say.

Patty wipes her face with a soaked sleeve.

You had that coming. Now mop up all that water and start again.

Chosen

At the edge of
the yard at St. Anthony Elementary
sun splinters
a girl-woman holding a child

they're suffused with light,
like those Madonnas cradling
infant gods, their full-body
plaster haloes. Her belly's
high and round, breasts
soft balloons, runaway hair

Grade 8 girls, not quite
flat-chested, not quite
whispering *It's Coreen*

my sister, says Coreen
frayed grey blanket
scent of too-much baby
powder

Grade 8 girls pulling away
bunch of hicks, one yelled
when we got off the bus

the baby's head
tinge of cinnamon
corn-silk

on Coreen's lower eyelash
the tear the shepherd children saw
on the Lady of Fatima
who, on the eve of war,
wheeled the sun
dazzled the unrepentant sky

Coreen crosses the street
straight-backed
up the steps of the rooming-house

Tess and Her Child (1973)

a toddler

in red, the kind that clings
to your tongue
after cinnamon candies

he high-steps, as though
his small feet are weights,
grasps chairs for balance

a slim white rope winds
through the furniture
in a wide circle, encloses him.

      I wait outside the rope

Tess, his mother, my schoolmate,
returns from the narrow
bedroom in the far corner

her hair tied back, not
radical, angled cheekbone
to chin like before

in her arms, she holds
the textbooks, almost new   the toddler
clambers up her leg

      I hand the cash over the rope

Tess's books—Grade 12 Biology,
The Crucible, As You Like It
she wishes me luck

I fill my lungs with air

leave her and the toddler
kenneled there

Tess and Her Child (1988)

Tess told him
his seafood allergy was a fluke,
his long thighs from the men on her side,
the freckles strewn across the tops of his hands
a trick of the August heat.

She told him
his gift for checkers was thanks to his grandmother,
who taught him before he moved here.

She told him
she couldn't find the photos of him
in his first two years. That carton got lost.

She told him
when he was a toddler, his father
crooned Springsteen, danced him to sleep
in the dark.

She told him
don't race into romances
girls—their dance-floor moves.

The day she screamed,
he pinning the dog down on the family-room carpet,
she told him
gentlemen never play rough.

She told him
his real father could not be reached.
The man who'd gone. Too far.

Glory

Women, St. Paul says, are the glory of man, since they are made from the body of man. I learned this at sixteen. A woman is not made in the image of God. She has to hide her failing by covering her head in church.

Her hat makes her eligible to pray in God's presence. Therefore, a parade of hats in my teens: straw boaters, berets, cloches, wide-brims, haloes (my mother knew all the names). But we girls wanted no hats at all, especially in summer. It must have been a devout women's libber who trimmed white lace into a simple oval and called it a chapel cap. White bobby pins recommended. Not really a hat, but we could get away with it. Once, I forgot my cap. I made do with a tissue, and a bobby pin the colour of housefly.

Don't, my mother said, *there will be consequences.*

My father didn't dance. He'd stuff his feet into his good shoes, joke that he knew a man who had died on the dance floor. At a wedding, Mom danced with her brother. *Flatfooted, tongue-tied, dummkopf*—I bet my father flung words like that at himself, while the fiddler's bow see-sawed. He wouldn't speak to her for days.

I Could Say

I was seventeen, coat-check girl at a downtown Oktoberfest. A country girl in the city. I could say I hid the hot pants under my dress.

I could say this was an unspeakable trauma from my past.

I noticed the man behind the reception desk noticing me. I wished I had heels instead of flats.

The waitresses wore dirndls, their skirts like bottomless birdcages. The men at the tables reached for those girls—what they were called then—as they passed cabbage rolls stuffed with meat.

The musicians wore suits. Men led sequined women about the dance floor. I thought of jeweled wedding dresses, although two of my cousins had cried on their way up the aisle.

I didn't like when he ran his hand like a ladle through my tip basket. I scooped the quarters into my purse.

But I liked leaving with him after the chandeliers went dark, the lobby empty and wanting. I was grateful for the ride to a girlfriend's.

I had the presence of mind to ask his name before I got into the car. Just V.K., he said, no one in this country can pronounce it anyway.

I savoured the meal at the roadhouse, baked potatoes slashed and topped with butter and cream.

I pitied the waitress. She was forty-ish, a black ring around one eye and a pair of slender wings tattooed on her clavicle. V.K. left no tip.

When he opened the car door, I slid in, charmed, purse on my thighs. He settled himself on the driver's side.

I was shocked when he thrust back the seat, gripped my neck. He smelled of meat, the meat of his mouth against my teeth. I struggled for breath.

I could say I saw a fist pound against his window. Say it was the waitress, eyes like struck matches, who made him stop.

Say the waitress held her arms out to me. If she was there at all.

Say I unburied my voice—muddy, grating—and flung myself out of the car.

Threshold

A flash, screech of metal
in the street outside
the coffee shop.

A car now hangs

dark in the air at our window
like a spaceship in *Star Trek*.

The driver, alone in her fatigue-
green, four-door Stratus,
her eyes large, fixed,
her face illegible.

And I am outside the lattice of time,
as I was that day on my uncle's farm
when I climbed a fence, gripped
its highest wire—electric. My hands,

my whole being, seized with low current.
I could not let go.
I could have poured myself,
effervescent, atomized,
into a free-form universe.

Velocity, mass, impact.
The car smashes into the shop,
stopped only by the stub
of wall under the window.

We huddle in a corner,
a man behind us grasps
my husband's shoulder.
We pick our way over glass shards.
Collect our belongings,

paltry things. Regulars
approach the counter.

On the sidewalk, a passing nurse,
like an extra on a set, helps
the driver out of her car.

She looks intact, like any young woman on the street.
And, as if we're at a dress rehearsal,
someone is sweeping,
broom bristles skimming the tops of our shoes.

Pro/Creation

I weighed it often
whether to carry a child
my mother carried nine
miscarried two, mourned

On her framed high-school diploma:

Latin
French
German
English
History
Geography
Geometry
Algebra
Trigonometry

Later, teacher's college, piano.

On her real-life plate:

bathing, peeling, weeding, pleasing
praying, mending, milking, canning
ironing, planting, picking
homework pies lunches
dog to feed, pickles to jar,
diapers to change, calves to wean

everything needed weaning

the little ones followed us girls around
as if they were our own

they were, in a way

one wouldn't sleep unless I lay down beside him
he'd wedge his body against me so he'd wake if I left him
the weight of them on our laps

Catholic girls who got caught
had to marry, live their error

unwed mothers gave birth
in a hospital wing for women mourning
stillborns
babies with defects

My father preferred my mother
not wear pants
not work off the farm
not read when he was in

My mother cleared my path
to university

I loved the library's affable hum
the spare study rooms
silent Mrs. Dalloway spaces

in class, Sartre and Joyce sieved the gravity
of catechism

Oh, ideas
bodiless
light
if tethered at all,
with a wisp of ink

I conceived, in my way

Each fall, students burst
into my classes, shining,
hungry. I had them
for eight months

Nieces, nephews bounded
abundant around me
I decided little ones were not imperative

I remembered
the swollen membrane in the barn gutter
milky, vein-blue balloon
I poked it
with a pitchfork tine just to see
the liquid, clear as rain,
leaked away in seconds

I noticed mothers and daughters
heads almost touching when they spoke
hands mirroring each other's

I saw
an old woman,
slight as a child,
cradled
from car to wheelchair
in a grown son's arms
a thrum in the blood
between them

on skin
the same cells divide, long
histories of touch survive

In her last gestation, my mother
caught mid-stride at dinner time—
her waters streamed down her legs
I was nine, holding the baby
who had learned late
how to wave goodbye

She, riding a salt wave,
its breaking, urgent,
primal, before-us.

The Ones Who Stay

Robin—Modern Literature.
For fourteen months, you carried
Camus to leukemia clinics,
showed me half-written papers,
your face swollen with drugs.
Soon I'll be finished, you'd say.
But the cure was too much.

*

David—Rhetoric and Writing.
On the day you withdrew
from college,
you, with your intrepid step,
traced the office maze
with your guide dog,
not once but twice, to find me.
Won't leave 'til I say goodbye.

*

Rod—Liberal Studies.
Every class, you baited and scowled,
chair shoved away from your desk,
waited for bit and bridle to drop.
At term's end, you strode to my table,
wordless, offered your hand.

*

Louise—Women's Studies.
We named the tyranny
of slender and smooth,
called up the radical, the loud,
the unpossessed. You, in your thirties,
uncovered your arm, mottled, ridged,
the one once scalded from shoulder to fist.

*

Mandy—Composition.
Your mom phoned from the hospital
after you'd missed all those classes.
You'd stopped taking your meds,
wandered the campus alone.
I still see you in the cold auditorium,
the café din, the far-off
bus shelter when it rains.

*

Jess—Philosophy.
Jess, who loved Plato,
Jess, her eyes Capella stars.
You remained between the ebb of one class
and the flood of the next,
my boyfriend says
get rid of it—
what do you think?

The Egtved Girl

Encountered on a trip to the National Museum of Denmark

Her corded-wool skirt, short,
the colour of peat. Her cropped top, a style
my niece would wear. The bronze belt-plate
a caught sun at her waist. I expected
to find the idea of her, a costume.

Her bones had dissolved, leaving
only scraps of teeth, tissue, nails
in the hollowed oak, her coffin.

She was sixteen, perhaps a German bride
pledged to a chief far from home. The Danes
buried her with care, wrapped her feet
against cold, her body in oxhide.
Gifted her with hairpins, honeyed beer.

I did not expect
the uterine pull from that mushroom-dark grave,
the rush of tenderness in my throat—
her hair, buttery waves where her face would have been.

The oxhide lay open
to expose the Girl's clothes, intact
but stained. I wanted to untangle
the woven strings of her skirt, untie
the round-backed antler comb on her belt
and place it in her hand.
Slip the small bracelets
onto child-like wrists.

I wanted to spread
the blanket that once covered her
over her ghost limbs. I wanted to unsee her,
uncovet her, give her privacy.

Above her hair, a swirl of wool
holds the ashes of a young child
in a birch-bark cup, bone
shards thin as fingernails.
Too charred to decode.

Had a child once lain
on her chest, in the place
where sorrowful Danes set
flowering yarrow?

I don't want to be told.
Let the Egtved Girl
—broken open, laid bare
for the last hundred years—
go on guarding
her secrets.

Counterpoint

In a west-coast studio,
I watch a student
in cut-back sneakers,
the ghost of a beard,
touch his cello's strings.
A pianist in black
hovers his hands above the keys,
ready at the charcoal grand.

In a garage in Boston,
a pair of young men
bend over a tarp
spread with parts, the usual bits
for pranks or science projects:
marbles, batteries, firecrackers.

The cellist glides his fingers,
draws his bow over the strings—
the notes fly as if from a bird's throat.

The youths in Boston
dig their hands
into a bag of finishing nails,
drop them into a pan
pour in BB shot, copper, zinc.
Metal pings on metal.

The pianist plays—
wind in summer leaves. His fingers
pleat air, speak the sibling keys.

The other two have tuned
spring-loaded valves, rotated the key,
snapped the switch from off to on.
Lashed their tools into backpacks.

The cellist's bow infuses the room—
the two unleash a vibrato
that lifts starlings into sky.

In Boston, the pair have broken time.
Dark rain, not flooding
but exploding,
in the sky. Flight
of debris, high-top shoe, Red Sox cap
metal twists, hair clip
the hand of a child.

Sisters at the Family Reunion

We've walked too long in shale light
like nuns bearing cracked relics at funerals,
elbows tight to our sides
to keep from touching.
We wear knitted caps with flaps
to muffle unkind words
or true ones.

The day, years ago, miles apart,
our words collided, ignited,
two power lines striking
in gale-force wind—
How many times have I
Why won't you see—
gunshot pop,
blue-green flash,
melt-metal heat.
Plunge into black.

But we don't want to part,
drop a guillotine blade
on the cord that binds us,
skipping rope, frayed ribbon,
shared soul-artery.
The nights, in thunderstorms,
we clung together
as if our small hearts leapt in one chest,
the lightning blazing our faces
onto each other's eyes.

What My Youngest Brother May Have Been Thinking as We Coloured at His Group Home

what if we are more
than a card trick by a rogue

chromosome: lobster iris
blue, Picasso guitar

more than a genus
slow-   tracked
in special classes

albino minds
latter-day lepers

what if we are more
than those typicals

whose synapses lunge
all at once
like greyhounds at the track

Bequest

My oldest brother farmed but raised no pigs.
He milked cows, worked fields, sired sons.
And a daughter. His life was husbandry.

He lay dying in hospital in harvest season,
his farm passed down to a son.
I sat with him, filled with feelings (love
was one), and he the same, I think.
The wide gravel yard still lay between us.
He pushed his IV between bed and window,
watched for his brothers. *The guys are coming
to get me in the dune buggy.*

A music therapist appeared.
He did not look at her when she said
his name. She placed an ocean
drum in the crook of his elbow,
guided his arm along its shallow round.
The sound the sea shushing over stones.
It was not a sound either of us had known.

But when she played the keyboard,
he sat up, hands gripping the drum,
tipped the pebbles inside one way,
then back to where they began.

The room swept clean with waves.

He turned to me, gave a slight bow,
handed me the drum. Sank
into the bright white sheets.

I tilted the drum, tried to play
what he had passed down,
a wordless song,
a priceless commodity.

Two Polaroids

Home early from school,
quiet in the summer kitchen,
I saw, for the first time,
my parents embrace,
lips, jaws, arms softening
like ice cream in August.

The other time, at the hospital
when my father failed
to recall the clock's face—
him, seated on the cot,
my mother standing,
holding him.

What She Might Have Dreamed the Night before I Took Her to the Home

A green light—it's damn well time. The stick shift hard in the claw of my hand. Past the church windows I've cleaned. Snuffed candles. Forgive me my trespasses. Light by green light, I reel in the main drag like a clothesline, a white flag at the far end. *Edie, give her hell,* Earl used to shout, and I am, but not in the diesel cloud of a tractor mired up to the axle. Him pushing from behind, and then giving it to me when the metal beast slid deeper. Tonight I'm in my daughter's sportscar. Blessed is the fruit of my womb. My daughter at the neighbour's with a thank-you gift. High-tech binoculars. All that watching out for me deserves some reward. *I've heard it's best you not drive, Mom, you don't want to hurt anyone.*

I brake hard at the T intersection. Earl bracing in the doorway like a cop when I told him I'd found work. And me backing down. Holy Mary, Mother of God, pray for me. *Best you don't cook, Mom, you don't want to forget and leave the burner on.* Him shoving his plate at me when the eggs ran. *Best you not sing in the choir, Mom, your heart won't take those steps.* Him calling me to come up as I folded the shirts below. My daughter circling the stacks of boxes in my flat, her voice on the phone—*She's not well*—echoing.

The Buck

The buck in our yard. So grand I want
to write an ode for him. His rack—

implacable—a first-Viking crown,
towering, tined, trophy. Forked, as though

it might divine silver, ruby, deep
spring waters, other-world rivers.

All this on a slender head, muzzle brushed
satin. Sometimes he lies down,

stretches his neck along the ground,
rests his chin on the grass. Oh, the weight,

the weight of his title. Larger than most,
limbs fine-boned, lethal. Haunches

whitened. Today, while he grazes,
a front leg, bloodied at the knee,

dangles. The other legs bewildered.
His eyes, unblinking, follow us when

we cross the gravel driveway. We speak
in low tones, let him be, veiled

by old rhododendrons, canopied
by aucuba, abutilon. Enough

water in the fountain, clover in the lawn.
He inclines his rack toward the far horizon.

The Imminence of Fracture

My left hand, ... my thinking hand, must be relaxed, sensitive. The rhythms of thought pass through the fingers and grip of this hand into the stone. It is also a listening hand. It listens for ... flaws in the stone; for the ... imminence of fractures.

—Barbara Hepworth, sculptor

Marble changes colour, depending on the hands that touch it.

White has claimed the back of my husband's head.

My father lies in the recliner, lists his children's names again and again.

A man creeps down the highway in the dark, painting the cracked centre line.

An elephant enslaved for fifty years cries when freed from his shackles.

At the edge of the Acropolis, giant toads leap and bark in the Cave of Pan.

Some shadows are deeper than concavity.

Her carvings rise out of the land, spheres and hills, spirals and valleys.

A woman walks the road, presses against the wind, her body wrapped in a shawl.

VIA FEMMINILE

Via Femminile I
A Woman Refuses a Suitor

In Catania, women lay white cakes
on silver platters—it's St. Agatha Day.
Everyone in pale sackcloth, black berets
for the town's early-Christian virgin,
who vowed *To God I am consecrated.*

Agatha declined a man at her peril.
She was taken prisoner. Fed crushed cakes.
Iron pincers burned and shredded her breasts.
An earthquake—oh miracle—stayed her death,
her red veil unscathed in the hot-coal bed.

Today her ceramic statue rides in litters
decorated with moonstone roses, faux gold,
shy cherubs waving crosses. They pass cherry-
stained windows. There Agatha's placid likeness
carries her breasts, intact, on a silver platter.

Along the route, the faithful praise this patron
of rape victims, wet nurses, bellfounders.
They light five-foot candles, carry her veil.
They feast on *Minni di Virgini*—iced white
mounds, cherry-topped, served on silver platters.

Via Femminile II
A Woman Lays Her Cloak on Hollow Seas

A woman of a certain age should not carry frankincense.
The mirror should not bear the gravity of her reflection.
In the bread she should hide coins from passing magicians.
She should not dry her husband's feet with her hair,
should shun glass slippers, olive branches, quiet churches.
She should not fold fig leaves into the winding sheets,
nor lower the pail into the dark cavity of the village well.

Let her place her ear on the belly of an ancient doe,
hear the cry of a newborn from a far-off moon,
lay her cloak on the salt dunes of hollow seas,
breathe her knowing on the cloth till water breaks.

Via Femminile III
A Woman Meets Her Captors' Eyes

she glides free   salt-water stream   birth-blood current   rapture love
rush   her first syllable

Nurses scrub her clean of mother-fluids, wrap her in flannel.
Record birth date: 2002.

she feeds   mouth   breast   milk   breast   mouth

In public, she suckles only in designated areas, face and nipple veiled.

on the ice at ten   she darts, holds, surges, scores   makes the boys'
team

She sits on the bench, sees the boys win.
Outside the dressing room, she hears them hoot and chant.

In high school, her male teacher measures her
skirt under the boys' gaze. She passes
this test, but fails the next—she reveals too much
collarbone. She reports to detention with other "girls."

she starts a petition   leads a demonstration   makes demands
forges change

she plays varsity soccer   posts her best kick   how it blue-skies

Women on campus slut-shame her
over and over on her phone's screen—
"she's whoring herself out," showing too much thigh.

she reads   Winnie Mandela   dissident 1969   held naked in solitary
Winnie lets her flow run down her legs   meets her captors' eyes

the young woman posts another soccer photo   leg flung high

Via Femminile IV
A Woman Uproots a Thistle

The day after he left

she ran her tongue along her teeth,
expected a gap.

She dreamed she flung a grapple to the far side of a gorge,
it clawed the air, dropped over a mile into the rift.

A week after he left

she stopped wearing his mustard cardigan,
the one he couldn't stretch over his waist.

She tore out the milk thistle he'd grown for his prostate,
shot each prickled stalk at the compost heap—didn't miss.

A month after he left

she built a gravel bioswale across the yard,
after seven rains, the lawn leapt, free of toxins.

Via Femminile V
Women Mend

Imagine borders torn asunder
while women glide needles up, under,
thread front, back, north and south together.
Imagine borders. Torn asunder,
fallen lands pinned on maps in war rooms.
Quilt stitches join patches bright as fields—
imagine! Borders sundered, sundered
while women glide needles up, under.

Via Femminile VI
A Woman Voices the Dark

Her vocal cords taut
voice a bell
trussed in a tower

Her voice *the dark
fields of tongue,
the red-blond speakings*

Her voice the rise and fall
of breath, the valley
of road, rise of cliff

Her voice a thumb on sternum
blood coursing, Gregorian,
as if water drumming

Her voice the earth path
between shelter and the she-wolf
kindred, electric.

Via Femminile VII
A Woman Is Found

Bulbous breasts, swollen belly, enormous vulva. Ice Age fertility figure.

Oolitic, made from a stone egg the size of an infant head. She fits easily into a hand.

In 1908, archaeologists don't want to call her Venus. This limestone stub from Willendorf, Austria. This bit of gravel.

Did hunters carve this goddess by the fire at night?

By day, perhaps she clung to the inside of a pocket as they gave chase. Wild horses plunging over the Stranska cliffs.

She was found naked except for bracelets on negligible wrists, arms kindling sticks resting on breasts. Her feet, thick toes.

Oh, and a hat. Nubbled, like the surface of a golf ball. Or knitted, like a toque for winter. Or an upside-down basket, pulled over her nose?

She is blinded. Unless you count a nearby pock mark an eye.

A goddess must not be seen, a scholar states.

Ice-age fertility goddesses surfaced in Danube alluvia, scattered like ghosts in settlements, near dark stains where hearths may have been. Hidden in dwellings, buried in small pits. Safeguarded.

Perhaps carved by women, who, looking down at their own bodies, rendered accurately the fullness of breasts, the round of belly in the last trimester. The eye of navel. Women born from an egg, and still of it—

Painted with red ochre, colour of blood, of menses, and birth.

This Venus is cleaned before being placed in a museum. Like a newborn purged of mother-fluids, a woman scrubbed after bleeding.

Residue of ochre in the creases of navel, vulva, breast. Red, yes, but more. Rubio root, scarab ink, Hestian fire.

SEEDBED

Homecoming

The leaves of the harvest table
lie in the dark apple cellar.

I draw his painted chair up to the wood stove.
Girls' winter hankies once charred in the flames.

Jade tree, ancient, mute on the stoop.
Peonies lean on the rail, too laden to stand.

Outside, the church spire beyond evergreens.
The Angelus peals, three strokes times three.

Stubble, bleached pale in August fields, forgets
to dream of wheat.

Elegy

Like one of those closed-eyed dolls,
dear youngest brother, you lie at rest.
The knot between your eyebrows
unlaced. You could be meditating, your gaze
inward, not looking out through thick lenses,
those gone, along with nebulizer, care worker.

Your grown-man shoulders, teen waist.
Fingers like a Raphael Sistine cherub's.
The undertaker places a stuffed mouse beside you.
You would have loved its soft sheen.

You arrived in March,
tiny triangle of tongue lying
on your lower lip, your limbs bluish, weighty,
like garden earth turned too early in spring.
We peered into the crib, Mom turned away,
prayed we wouldn't notice—or hoped we would—

You were her quiet child, passed from her lap to ours
and back, patient, watching, eyes like the blue
shards of glass I'd find in clay furrows behind Dad's
plough—

You walked—we finally let you—ran, elfin
after big brothers, gamboling dogs, spindly foals,
diffident felines: each one paused until you caught up.

When we fell silent, you talked:
hockey games, coffee shops, blonde girl-singers.
You were a man.
You danced non-stop at weddings.
At the end, legs like halting canes.

Now, on your forehead, a spot,
like a coin, from where you fell face down
that night: not Lenten ash, nor last-rites oil.
This wound borne on your way
from here to that unknowable there.

Remembering Fields Where Fathers and Uncles Fought
—or Spring Planting

Repatriation of fallen Canadian soldiers from Germany to Groesbeek Cemetery, Gelderlands, the Netherlands

1

Fall, 1947. The grass vibrant. Temporary white crosses, row on row, have sprung up on the graves like scarecrows. On each cross, the same details: Number: *C. 122705*. Rank: *Private*. Name: *W.B. Brown*. Regiment: *Algonquin*. Date of Death: *9-4-45*. Later, tablets meant to stay would give an age: *19*. And an epitaph: *"The voice we loved is still, the chair is vacant in our home and can never be filled."*

Today, the cemetery unveiling. The fallen are assembled, at rest. The ones not found memorialized on limestone plaques. 1,103. A young hedge still in full leaf. Children in knee socks at the edge of each grave. The bereaved gather on the gravel that runs up the middle of the field. At the front, a queen and her prince seated with generals.

On a dias, a priest, white surplice against a flint sky, prays for the deceased. Behind him a stone cross reaches up twenty feet. The Cross of Sacrifice. On it, a longsword, blade down, hangs where Christ's body would be.

Allied flags at full mast. Now a bugler plays, the flags descend. The queen places a wreath at the foot of the cross. The generals salute. In unison, the children bend, set bouquets on the graves. Cut flowers.

April, 1946.   a hilltop field

its edge, maize, fallen   lodged in mud   stubble broken

                    ankle   bone

          debris cut   harrow's teeth

          the rest clean, even   loam   moist   fertile

                    ground   opened

Piles of dirt heaped   right of the holes   unifor

seven-foot coffins   green grey   to th left

Inside   remains unearthed in battlefields   silent—

Rhin lan   Elbe   Maas   Seine   Scheldt

found   where   grass grew vivid   water   brackish

olive drab   puttees belt

          badge   cutlery   jaw b ne

Today 101 coffins laid deep   cov red.

scrape of shovels   drop of clay on planed poplar   To orrow the same.

And the next twen -four days 2,238 Canadi so iers

retur ed to rest in th "fr dly land they had died to s ve.

side by ide, in egimen s, as thoug called to attention for a last ti hey f ce t enem to   south

cres of burial g   soothe   spring br ze.

no Ca dian li b   in emy so l

In the fall, when the field is spent, let it fallow. Let the bled earth sleep, like a womb after birth, like the sea at its lowest ebb. Let stubble hoard the snow, free of plough-share blade and half-moon hoof. In the spring, let April nurse the ground, soft, with rain, then wind from the south. Cast alfalfa seed over the land; let its pea-shoots quicken, its heart buds bloom. Let the green green. Just past its youth, strike it down and turn it underneath. Blood of the lamb. Let the season pass, and the field will renew.

Earthquake

Ten days after my mother's funeral

> the earth heaved
> beneath me,
> two thousand miles
> from her grave

> deep-throated,
> wave-
> shearing, rock-
> twisting, leviathan.

Had she risen from her death sleep,
lashed free

shucked the buttoned-up
Christian-Mother dress
for pants the green of wheat grass

shucked the tangled hippocampus,
the mean limits of casket geography?

Did she raise her voice
get cracking, Peter,
lead me through those gates?
Did the beads from her rosary,
once wrapped around her hands,
scatter like
seeds
when she gesticulated?

Or did she churn and twist

in that satin
coffin sleeve,
as she had in her dying bed,
grasping the side rails,
sheets winding around her?

That baritone
rumble is the earth's
mantle, itself held captive,
rocking her in its warm
iron arms.

Visitation

In cascading November rain
we five sisters stand on a Tofino beach
storm-shielded in Gore-Tex suits
old sorrows pressing like backpacks on our scapula.

My mother, dead two years

her hands light as wings on our hair
loosening the ties under our chins
brushing waterproof hoods from our heads
ferrying us all
to a rainforest afloat with bright
leaves greening

She lifts us away from winter
wind in our eyes
mist shape-shifting, waves
piling one on the next
sea-breath sighing
someone a thousand miles away
calling
in a voice that carries us
to another time, to this beard-lichen gate
where we are almost-teens
loose-limbed in pedal pushers
canvas sneakers.

*

Suffused in new-June sun,
we bike through cedars
the peat soft beneath our wheels
she bikes too   we see her
for the first time cycling
as she did in black-and-white snapshots scattered
in her hope chest

She stops, sets her bike aside
she is almost-old, hair speckled black and white,
a loon's back   she is almost-young, face lit
with first-glimpse wonder, smile puckish

she raises her hand
not to rebuke, but conspire
as if to say, *Wait, you won't believe it*
we abandon our bikes, surround her, transfixed.

                                        *

She drinks in what we cannot see: licorice-
fern scent, flicker of waxwing
she lowers her hand   a shaft of light
springs from her palm, arches into the trees
for a moment unseen
then, like a cosmic skipping rope, falls
toward the earth   she, arm turning
without effort, says *Jump in*

                        When we leap into that rope of light
yellow green magenta blue spill down
as though the Milky Way has unfolded
let a billion stars descend, bursting
light-blooms showering
our faces, our chests, our soul-bruises

                        On the beach
                                summer-warm, we
particles tumbling, jubilant, just born
our bodies before body, translucent
blue of the sea

                                and she, a shimmer
in the pink of our beginnings.

How to Live Edge-wise

1

When I'm ancient,
will I sit at my bay window
each day? The glass
a sealed aperture.
Let's age in place,
my husband will say,
dying soon after.

Go outside, I'll tell myself,
go outside. No potatoes
to peel, no silence cloth to iron.
A rogue wind coming, maybe.

One summer night,
I'll squint through
a spangled cataract
to see Orion's stars
flashing blue and red.

Peer into
the galaxy edge-wise,
the scientists say.
The Milky Way, 75,000
light years wide.

Thirteen billion years old,
it gathers agèd stars, still radiant,
in its spiral arms.

2

I'll feed the scarlet hummingbird
cane sugar in spring water.

Each day, it must eat as much as it weighs.

Its beaked ancestor lives on
in its hollow bones.
The three-toed therapod.
The bird's body like my own
heart, if it rose above
its faulty beat.

3

I'll walk down Midland Road
to build stamina.

Where I lived as a child,
Jesuit priests were massacred
in a place called Midland.

In a painting at home,
these men floated, haloed,
above the village they'd inflamed.

Some died by slow-fire torture.
When one priest did not plead,
his captors ripped out his heart,
drank his blood for courage.

On the way home,
I'll gaze through the steel grate
of a storm drain,
watch Bowker Creek
buck and foam underground,
even when it can't escape.

4

I'll come in through the basement,
past the clouded window
etched with caught poppies.
Find it's too close inside.

I'll go back out, gaze
up toward Betelgeuse,
Orion's supergiant star.

We two will burn red with age.
We will explode—
ghost-light the cosmos.

Not a Pretty Stone

In Gros Morne Park,
I come upon a rock, broken, strange.
One side cracked black, mixed with rust-red
and cream. The other, rippled crystal, back-lit green,
as if shed from a distant planet.

Peridotite,
                  Earth's mantle.

Mammoth curtain-wall between surface and
core, that molten heart.

Conductor of rising magma and cooling stone,
tectonic drag and volcanic flare,
forge of common iron and olivine gem.

It lines ragged rifts in the deep-sea floor

                  until the ocean crust, in a wild heave, thrusts

                          above the continental plate

instead of sliding below.

        Mantle bursts into air for the first time.

              Its green glimmers of primal sea   for a geological breath

before weather crackles the rock into dull serpentine.

I hold the scrap in front of me—
fire, earth, water, jewel.
Blood-blush rising in my hands.

Taking the Waters 2

I sit poolside
out of the sun.

Under my dress, dark polyester suit
with bra shelf.

Mira, slight, fifteen,
in her sea-green bikini.

Her left arm bare, the right
in an emerald lycra sleeve. Underneath,
old cuts, like minnows clinging
when a predator is near.

She leaps from the pool's edge,
slices the water. Glides under
like a creature washed clean
in the balm of its river.

      My brothers, leaping
that hot evening, loose-
limbed, naked,
into the peat-black creek.
Non-swimmers imagining
their limbs swimming.
They whooped, crowed, splashed
—white bodies like poltergeists
in the dusk.
I crouched, forbidden,
in the corn field and saw

      their joy

           their risk

               the dark energy between their legs.

Me in the creek once—at a kids' picnic.
In the noon glare, in my aunt's maroon
one-piece suit. Standing in silt-water
up to my neck to hide the swellings
on my chest. I gripped my toes on round
stones in the creek bed's ooze.
Imagined how to lift my body to float—
the stone under my left foot reared.
I bled.

In the pool, Mira surfaces,
cropped hair wet, purple
water-iris bloom.

She stretches her arms high.
Her sheathed arm a jeweled banner.
She has re-imagined shame.

She rises, gleaming, to the deck.
Lithe, she walks on tiptoes, noiseless.
On her thighs, rows of short scars,
a faded inventory.

The water is clear.
I dive in.

AFTERWORD

The series of poems entitled Via Femminile (the Path of Women) is inspired by the Christian Via Crucis (the Way of the Cross, the path of suffering). The Way of the Cross is represented by a group of images depicting the suffering and patience of Christ as he carries the cross to the site of his crucifixion. These images, represented by plaques, crosses or small paintings, are named as chapters in a book might be: "Jesus falls a second time," "Simon of Cyrene helps Jesus carry the cross."

In the week before Easter, parishioners, led by their priests, re-enact this journey on a pilgrimage through their church or along an outside route. They stop in front of each image, reflect and pray. The Way of the Cross ends with Jesus's death, or in some versions, with his Resurrection. The women in the Via Femminile poems are, for the most part, not deities, but ordinary women. As a collective, they have borne discrimination and violence, yet have survived, thrived.

The italicized words in "Via Femminile VI—A Woman Voices the Dark" are from Tim Lilburn's poem "The Dark Fields of the Tongue," published in his collection *Kill-site*.

NOTES

Acknowledgement is gratefully extended to the editors of following literary journals and anthologies in which several of these poems first appeared: *CV2, FreeFall, Heart of Wisdom: Life writing as Empathic Inquiry, Island Writer, Poems from Planet Earth, Prairie Fire, Room, Wordworks.*

Some of these poems are included in a video for Poets Caravan, a series created by Victoria's Planet Earth Poetry.

"What She Might Have Dreamed the Night before I Took Her to the Home" first appeared in the chapbook *What Else Could I Dare Say*, edited by Patrick Lane and published by Leaf Press in 2011.

The poem "Counterpoint" was written in response to the bombing at the Boston marathon in April 2013.

The epigraph in "The Imminence of Fracture" is a quotation from Barbara Hepworth, taken from her book *A Pictorial Autobiography*. The poem is inspired, in part, by Hepworth's sculptures and writings. Hepworth died in a fire at her studio in 1975.

The three-part poem entitled "Remembering Fields Where Fathers and Uncles Fought" is inspired by the palimpsest. A palimpsest is an original text over which another text has been written. When seventh-century scribes washed away unwanted writing from their parchment, a faint residue of earlier writing sometimes appeared. In early medieval books, the more recent text ran perpendicular to the effaced text, as shown in Poem 3. The deepest layer in these texts might be a page from Middle-Age agricultural manuals.

ACKNOWLEDGEMENTS

I gratefully acknowledge that the land on which I live is the traditional territory of the Coast and Straits Salish Peoples. I thank the Lekwungen People, known today as the Songhees and Esquimalt Nations, and recognize that their historic connections to these lands continue to this day.

My deep thanks to

the outstanding mentors who led retreats and workshops I attended, especially Patrick Lane and Lorna Crozier, whose transcendent poetry and teaching astonished me, and continue to enrich my writing.

the many poets I have come to know at retreats, workshops, and Victoria's Planet Earth Poetry; their genius and camaraderie are great gifts.

spirited Wendy Donawa, for making this poetic journey a joy; and Arleen Paré, for her quiet wisdom and steadfast faith in my writing.

my poetry group—Ulrike Narwani and Gisela Ruebsaat—for inspired reviews and generous encouragement.

Michelle Mulder and Lynne Van Luven for their candid and bountiful support; and Lynne Mustard, for lively poetry talks over tea.

Yvonne Blomer and Carla Funk, who guided me energetically and inventively as my collection evolved.

Cornelia Hoogland, for showing me how to break open my manuscript and find the light inside: such brilliance and fierce belief.

Anita Lahey, who edited this collection with extraordinary acuity and care.

Caitlin Press—Vici, Sarah, and Malaika—for producing and championing this book with skillfulness, enthusiasm, and grace.

my family and friends who unstintingly cheer me on; and the bookies, who light up my days with their open hearts and passion for literature.

my sisters and brothers: how richly we are tied to each other by blood, field, story—and our shy but abundant love.

And immeasurable gratitude to Gary, whose amazing love and humour sustain me when I'm writing, and always.

ABOUT THE AUTHOR

Susan Braley grew up in a family of eleven on a farm in Southern Ontario. Her life in this rural setting profoundly shaped her as daughter, sibling, feminist, partner, reader and writer.

Her poetry has appeared in literary journals such as *Antigonish Review, Arc Poetry Magazine, CV2, The Literary Review of Canada, The New Quarterly, Prairie Fire,* and *Room*; and in anthologies such as *Walk Myself Home* and *Poems from Planet Earth.* One of her poems appears in *Best Canadian Poetry 2023.* She was a nominee for the 2022 National Magazine Award for Poetry, and her poems have been recognized in numerous writing contests, including *Arc*'s Poem of the Year.

For much of her adult life, Susan lived in London, Ontario, where she earned a Ph.D. in Modern Literature, and taught literature and women's studies. She now lives in Victoria with her partner.